This book belongs to...

Sticker Times Tables for School

Written by Clare Gray
Illustrated by Ian Cunliffe

1 times table

Write in the missing numbers.

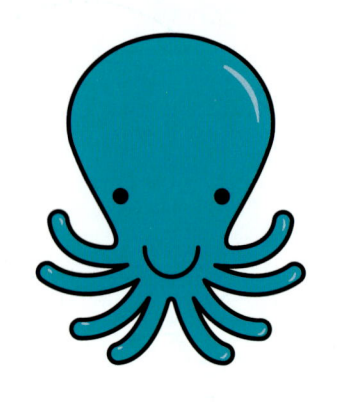

0 x 1 = 0
1 x 1 = 1
2 x 1 = 2
3 x 1 = 3
4 x 1 = 4
5 x 1 = 5

6 x 1 = 6
7 x 1 = 7
8 x 1 = 8
9 x 1 = 9
10 x 1 = 10

Now find the missing stickers to complete the number square.

1	2	3	4	5	6	7	8	9	10
11	12	13	14	15	16	17	18	19	20
21	22	23	24	25	26	27	28	29	30
31	32	33	34	35	36	37	38	39	40
41	42	43	44	45	46	47	48	49	50
51	52	53	54	55	56	57	58	59	60
61	62	63	64	65	66	67	68	69	70
71	72	73	74	75	76	77	78	79	80
81	82	83	84	85	86	87	88	89	90
91	92	93	94	95	96	97	98	99	100

Find the missing stickers, then tick or cross the boxes below to show whether each thing is in the main picture.

coconut ✓   banana ✓   fish ✗   crab ✓   man ✓   glass ✗

Now complete these sums.

9 x 1 = 9   3 x 1 = 3

5 x 1 = 5   6 x 1 = 6

1 x 1 = 1   4 x 1 = 4

2 times table

Write in the missing numbers.

0 × 2 = 0
1 × 2 = 2
2 × 2 = 4
3 × 2 = 6
4 × 2 = 8
5 × 2 = 10

6 × 2 = 12
7 × 2 = 14
8 × 2 = 16
9 × 2 = 18
10 × 2 = 20

Find the right stickers to finish the number square. Multiples of 2 are shaded.

1	2	3	4	5	6	7	8	9	10
11	12	13	14	15	16	17	18	19	20
21	22	23	24	25	26	27	28	29	30
31	32	33	34	35	36	37	38	39	40
41	42	43	44	45	46	47	48	49	50
51	52	53	54	55	56	57	58	59	60
61	62	63	64	65	66	67	68	69	70
71	72	73	74	75	76	77	78	79	80
81	82	83	84	85	86	87	88	89	90
91	92	93	94	95	96	97	98	99	100

2 socks make 1 pair. Add enough socks to make 4 pairs.
How many socks are there altogether?

2 x 4 = 8

Each bag has 2 handles. Add enough bags to make 12 handles.

5 x 2 = 12

Each bicycle has 2 wheels. Add enough bicycles to make 6 wheels.

3 x 2 = 6

Find the right cup sticker for each teapot.

7 x 2 =

5 x 2 =

2 x 9 =

2 x 10 =

3 times table

Write in the missing numbers.

0 x 3 = 0
1 x [3] = 3
2 x 3 = [6]
3 x 3 = [9]
4 x 3 = 12
5 x [3] = 15

6 x 3 = [18]
7 x [3] = 21
8 x 3 = 24
9 x 3 = 27
10 x 3 = [30]

Find the right stickers to finish the number square. Multiples of 3 are shaded.

1	2	3	4	5	6	7	8	9	10
11	12	13	14	15	16	17	18	19	20
21	22	23	24	25	26	27	28	29	30
31	32	33	34	35	36	37	38	39	40
41	42	43	44	45	46	47	48	49	50
51	52	53	54	55	56	57	58	59	60
61	62	63	64	65	66	67	68	69	70
71	72	73	74	75	76	77	78	79	80
81	82	83	84	85	86	87	88	89	90
91	92	93	94	95	96	97	98	99	100

Each alien has 3 eyes. Add enough aliens to the scene to make 15 eyes.

$3 \times 5 = 15$

Each planet has 3 rings. Add enough planets to the starry sky to make 9 rings.

$3 \times 3 = 9$

This space buggy has 3 wheels. Add enough space buggies to make 18 wheels.

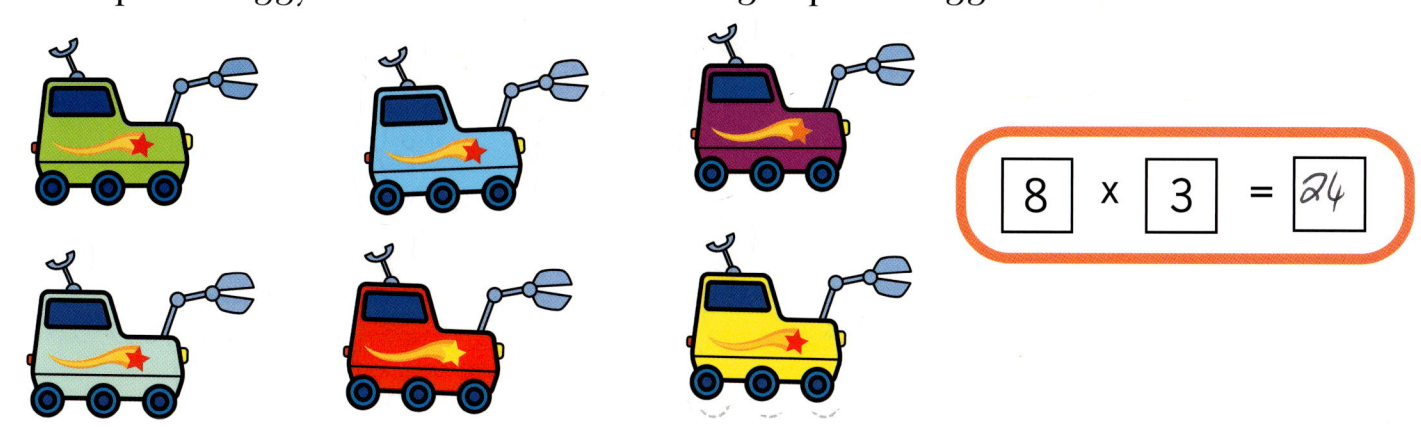

$8 \times 3 = 24$

Complete the alien sums.
Example: 3 antennae; 4 legs: 3 x 4 = 12

$3 \times 6 = 18$

$3 \times 8 = 24$

$3 \times 3 = 9$

4 times table

Write in the missing numbers.

0 × 4 = 0	6 × 4 = 24
1 × 4 = 4	7 × 4 = 28
2 × 4 = 8	8 × 4 = 32
3 × 4 = 12	9 × 4 = 36
4 × 4 = 16	10 × 4 = 40
5 × 4 = 20	

Find the right stickers to finish the number square. Multiples of 4 are shaded.

1	2	3	4	5	6	7	8	9	10
11	12	13	14	15	16	17	18	19	20
21	22	23	24	25	26	27	28	29	30
31	32	33	34	35	36	37	38	39	40
41	42	43	44	45	46	47	48	49	50
51	52	53	54	55	56	57	58	59	60
61	62	63	64	65	66	67	68	69	70
71	72	73	74	75	76	77	78	79	80
81	82	83	84	85	86	87	88	89	90
91	92	93	94	95	96	97	98	99	100

Each car has 4 wheels. Add enough cars to the road to make 16 wheels.

4 × 4 =

Each ship has 4 funnels. Add enough ships to the sea to make 24 funnels.

7 × 4 = 24

Each balloon has 4 passengers. Add enough balloons to the sky to make 12 passengers.

3 × 4 = 12

Find the right sticker for each lorry.

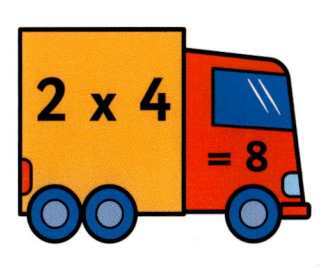

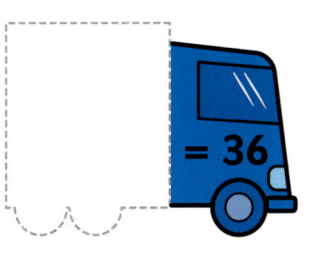

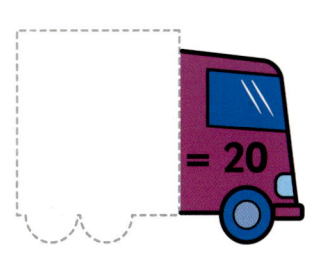

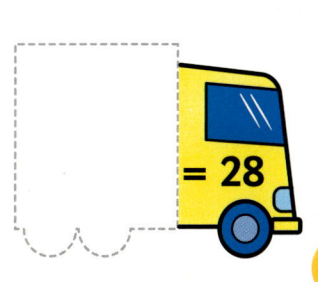

2 × 4 = 8   = 36   = 20   = 28

5 times table

Write in the missing numbers.

0 × 5 = 5
1 × 5 = 5
2 × 5 = 10
3 × 5 = 15
4 × 5 = 20
5 × 5 = 25

6 × 5 = 30
7 × 5 = 35
8 × 5 = 40
9 × 5 = 45
10 × 5 = 50

Find the right stickers to finish the number square. Multiples of 5 are shaded.

1	2	3	4	5	6	7	8	9	10
11	12	13	14	15	16	17	18	19	20
21	22	23	24	25	26	27	28	29	30
31	32	33	34	35	36	37	38	39	40
41	42	43	44	45	46	47	48	49	50
51	52	53	54	55	56	57	58	59	60
61	62	63	64	65	66	67	68	69	70
71	72	73	74	75	76	77	78	79	80
81	82	83	84	85	86	87	88	89	90
91	92	93	94	95	96	97	98	99	100

Each hen has 5 eggs. Add enough hens in the straw to make 25 eggs.

$\boxed{5} \times \boxed{5} = \boxed{25}$

Each cow has 5 spots. Add enough cows in the field to make 15 spots.

$\boxed{3} \times \boxed{5} = \boxed{15}$

Each rake has 5 prongs. Add enough rakes to make 30 prongs.

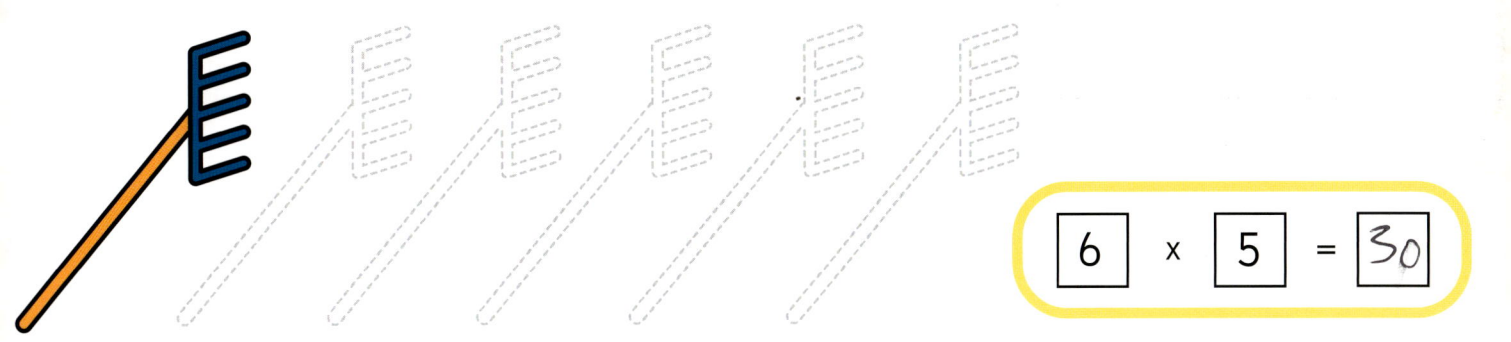

$\boxed{6} \times \boxed{5} = \boxed{30}$

Find the correct trailer stickers for each tractor.

6 times table

Write in the missing numbers.

0 x 6 = 6
1 x 6 = 6
2 x 6 = 12
3 x 6 = 18
4 x 6 = 24
5 x 6 = 30

6 x 6 = 36
7 x 6 = 42
8 x 6 = 48
9 x 6 = 54
10 x 6 = 60

Find the right stickers to finish the number square. Multiples of 6 are shaded.

1	2	3	4	5	6	7	8	9	10
11	12	13	14	15	16	17	18	19	20
21	22	23	24	25	26	27	28	29	30
31	32	33	34	35	36	37	38	39	40
41	42	43	44	45	46	47	48	49	50
51	52	53	54	55	56	57	58	59	60
61	62	63	64	65	66	67	68	69	70
71	72	73	74	75	76	77	78	79	80
81	82	83	84	85	86	87	88	89	90
91	92	93	94	95	96	97	98	99	100

1 times table – pages 2 - 3

2 times table – pages 4 - 5

21　62　45　87　18

3 times table – pages 6 - 7

4 times table – pages 8 - 9

52　23　66　97　28

7 times table – pages 14 - 15

21   45   81   70   8

8 times table – pages 16 - 17

3   41   56   89   92

56   64   72

9 times table – pages 18 - 19

81   76   3   90   27

9 times table – pages 18 - 19

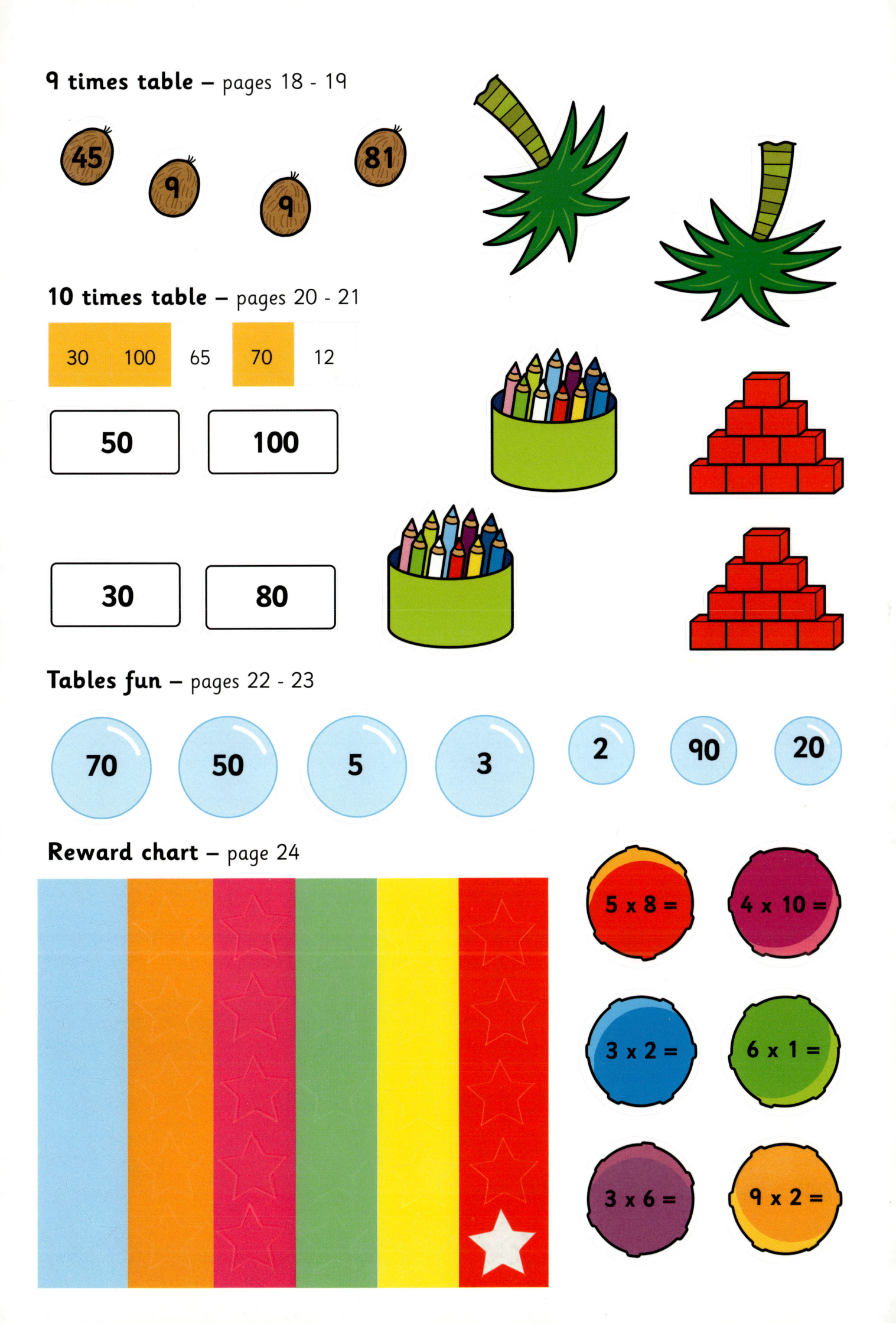

45   9   9   81

10 times table – pages 20 - 21

30 100 65 70 12

50   100

30   80

Tables fun – pages 22 - 23

70   50   5   3   2   90   20

Reward chart – page 24

5 x 8 =   4 x 10 =

3 x 2 =   6 x 1 =

3 x 6 =   9 x 2 =

5 times table – pages 10 - 11

13 65 95 58 90

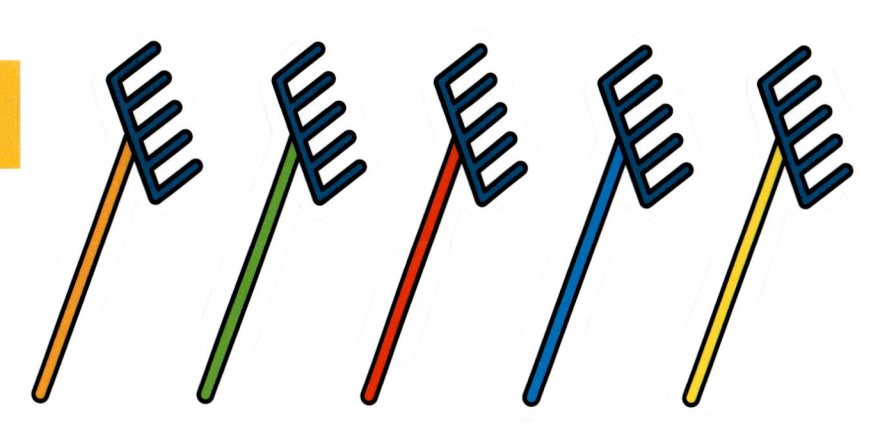

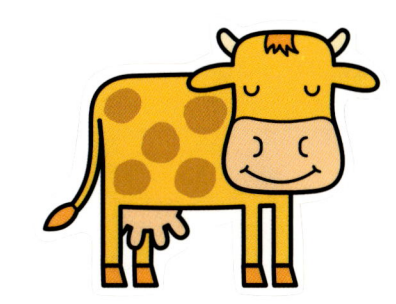

6 times table – pages 12 - 13

54 17 72 12 99

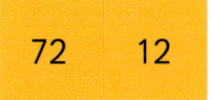

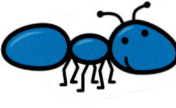

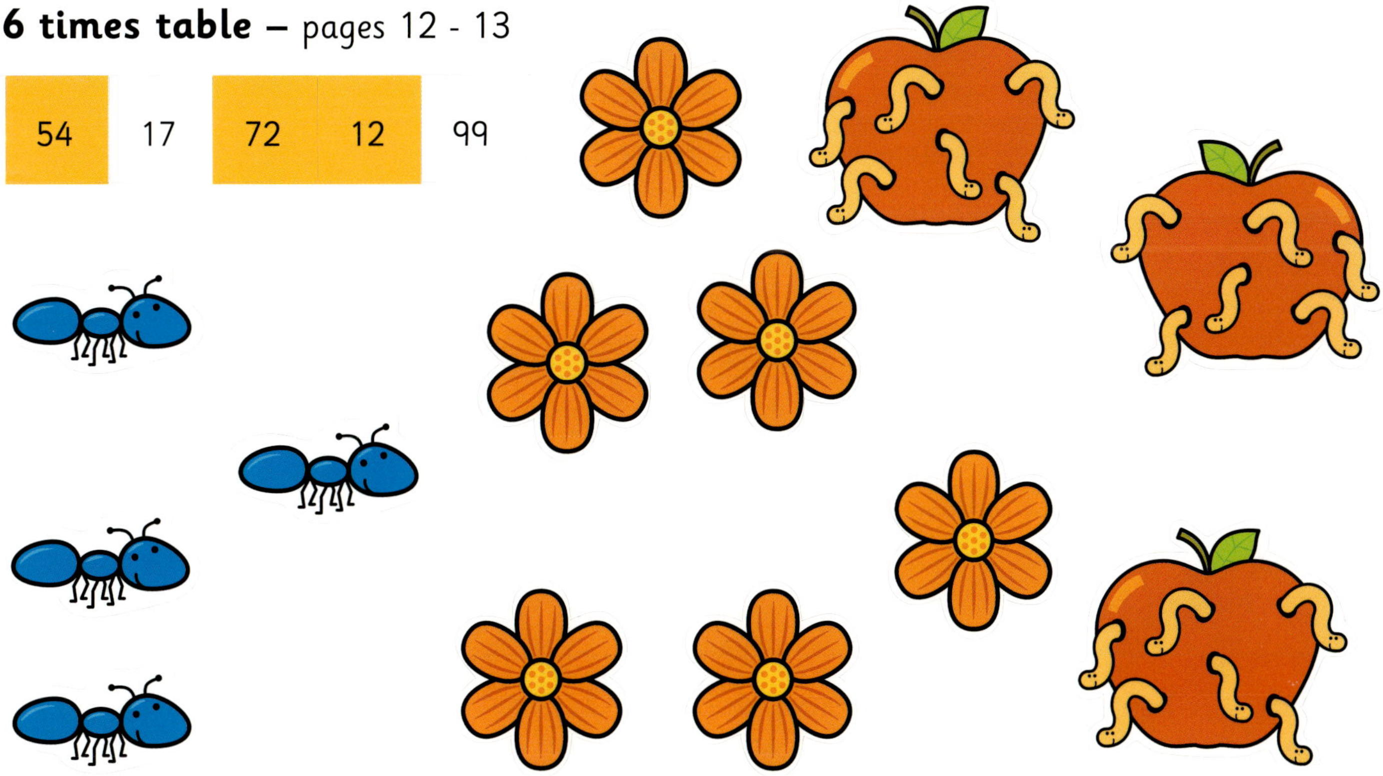

Each ant has 6 legs. Add enough ants to the trail to make 30 legs.

$\boxed{5} \times \boxed{6} = \boxed{36}$

Each flower has 6 petals. Add enough flowers to make 42 petals.

$\boxed{7} \times \boxed{6} = \boxed{42}$

Each apple has 6 worms in it. Add enough apples to make 24 worms.

$\boxed{4} \times \boxed{6} = \boxed{24}$

Every ladybird has 6 spots. Count the ladybirds on each leaf and fill in the blanks to show how many spots there are altogether.

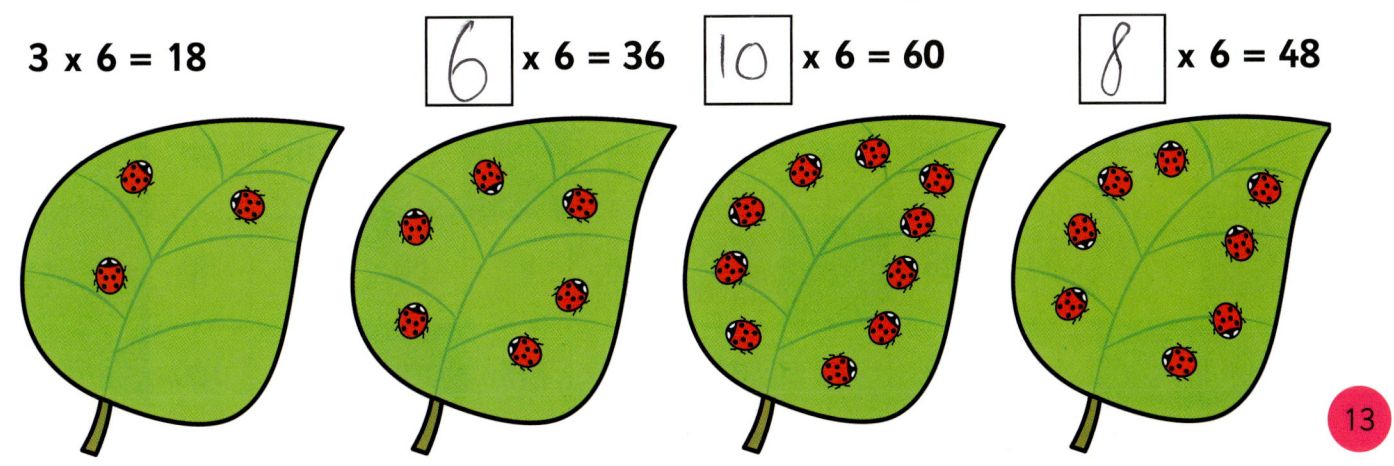

3 x 6 = 18 $\boxed{6}$ x 6 = 36 $\boxed{10}$ x 6 = 60 $\boxed{8}$ x 6 = 48

7 times table

Write in the missing numbers.

0 x 7 = 0
1 x 7 = 7
2 x 7 = 14
3 x 7 = 21
4 x 7 = 28
5 x 7 = 35

6 x 7 = 42
7 x 7 = 49
8 x 7 = 56
9 x 7 = 63
10 x 7 = 70

Find the right stickers to finish the number square. Multiples of 7 are shaded.

1	2	3	4	5	6	7	8	9	10
11	12	13	14	15	16	17	18	19	20
21	22	23	24	25	26	27	28	29	30
31	32	33	34	35	36	37	38	39	40
41	42	43	44	45	46	47	48	49	50
51	52	53	54	55	56	57	58	59	60
61	62	63	64	65	66	67	68	69	70
71	72	73	74	75	76	77	78	79	80
81	82	83	84	85	86	87	88	89	90
91	92	93	94	95	96	97	98	99	100

Each gingerbread man has 7 sweets on him. Add enough gingerbread men to make 35 sweets.

$\boxed{5} \times \boxed{7} = \boxed{35}$

Each jug can pour 7 glasses of squash. Add enough jugs to pour 49 glasses.

$\boxed{7} \times \boxed{7} = \boxed{49}$

Each cake has 7 candles. Add enough cakes to make 21 candles.

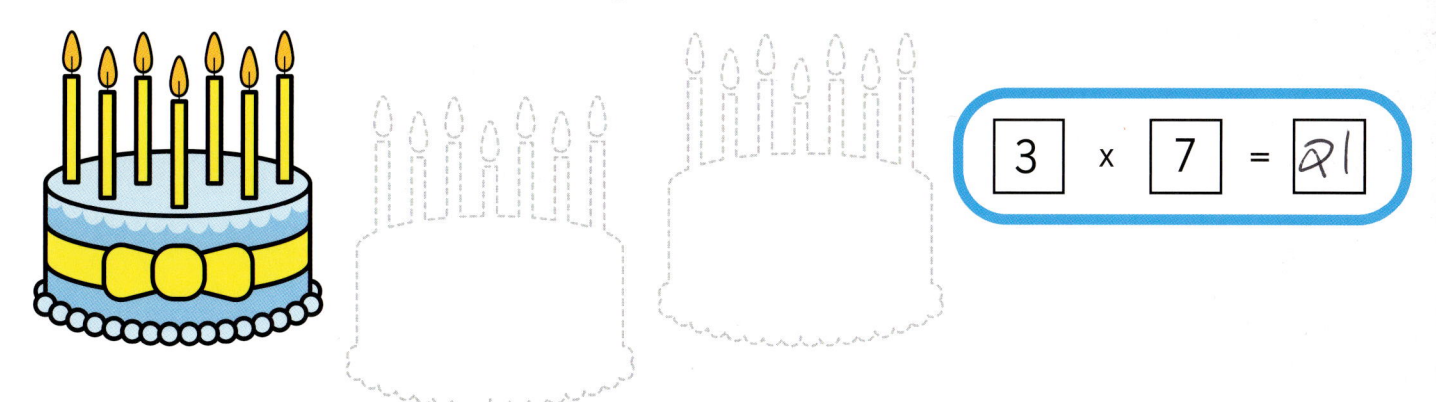

$\boxed{3} \times \boxed{7} = \boxed{21}$

BANG! 4 party poppers have exploded. Find the correct party popper for each question.

1 x 7 =   6 x 7 =   9 x 7 =   4 x 7 =

8 times table

Write in the missing numbers.

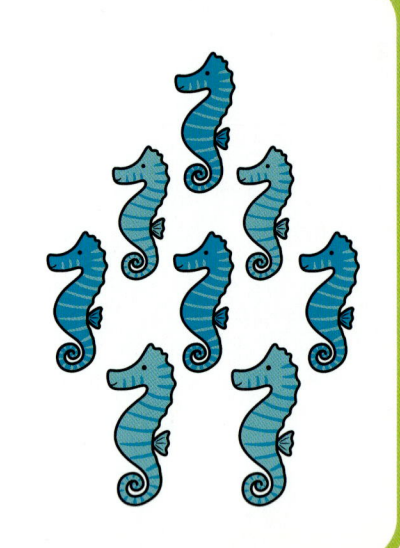

0 x 8 = 0
1 x 8 = 8
2 x 8 = 16
3 x 8 = 24
4 x 8 = 32
5 x 8 = 40
6 x 8 = 48
7 x 8 = 56
8 x 8 = 64
9 x 8 = 72
10 x 8 = 80

Find the right stickers to finish the number square. Multiples of 8 are shaded.

1	2	3	4	5	6	7	8	9	10
11	12	13	14	15	16	17	18	19	20
21	22	23	24	25	26	27	28	29	30
31	32	33	34	35	36	37	38	39	40
41	42	43	44	45	46	47	48	49	50
51	52	53	54	55	56	57	58	59	60
61	62	63	64	65	66	67	68	69	70
71	72	73	74	75	76	77	78	79	80
81	82	83	84	85	86	87	88	89	90
91	92	93	94	95	96	97	98	99	100

16

Each jellyfish has 8 legs. Add enough jellyfish to make 32 legs.

4 × 8 = ☐

Each seaweed plant has 8 leaves. Add enough plants to make 40 leaves.

5 × 6 = 40

Each submarine has 8 windows. Add enough submarines to make 24 windows.

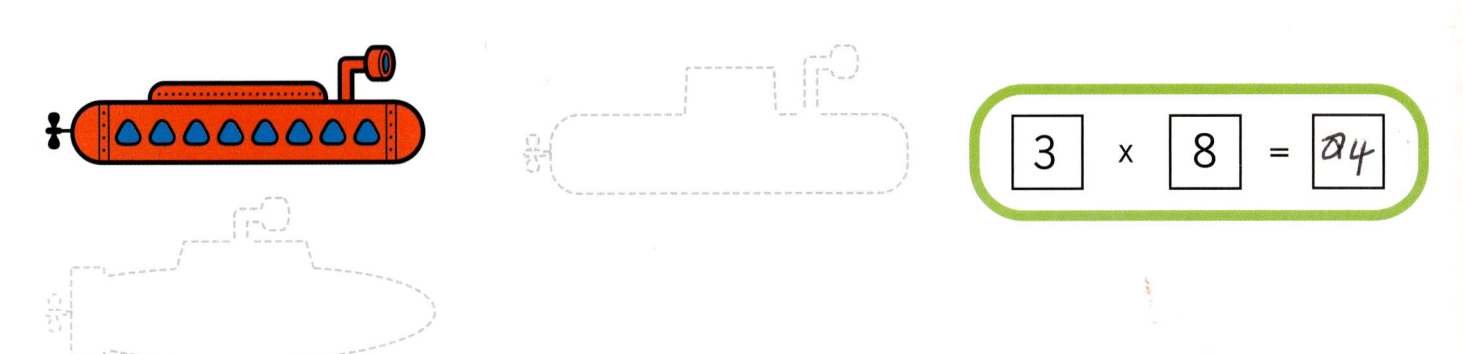

3 × 8 = 24

Find the correct bubble sticker for each fish.

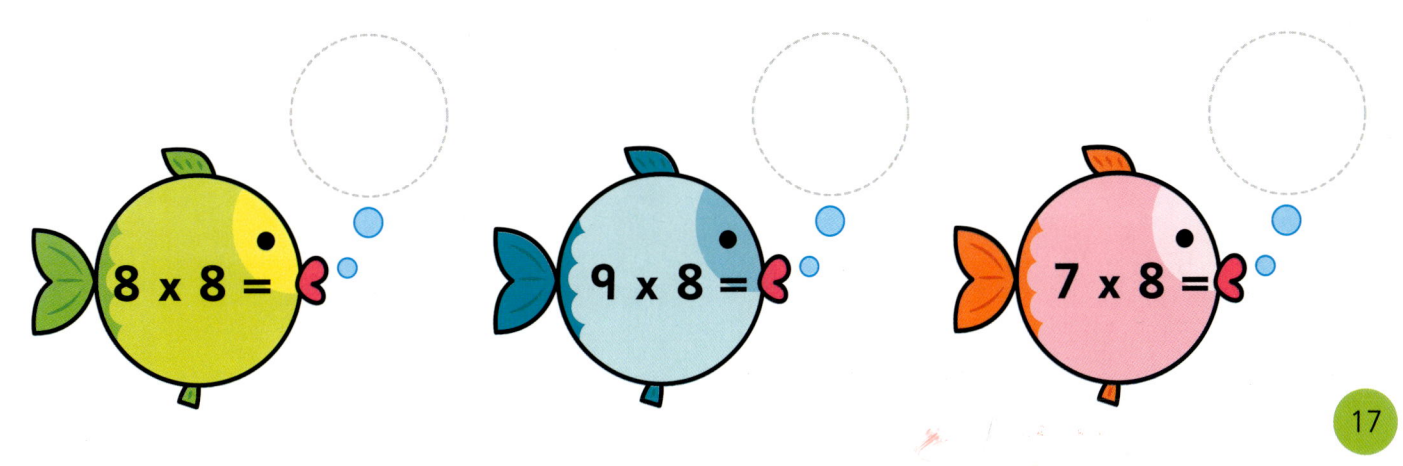

8 × 8 =

9 × 8 =

7 × 8 =

17

9 times table

Write in the missing numbers.

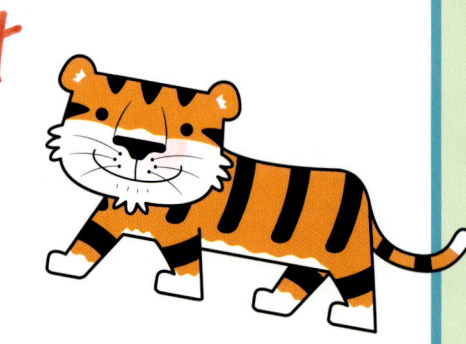

0 x 9 = 0	6 x 9 = 54
1 x 9 = 9	7 x 9 = 63
2 x 9 = 18	8 x 9 = 72
3 x 9 = 27	9 x 9 = 81
4 x 9 = 36	10 x 9 = 90
5 x 9 = 45	

Find the right stickers to finish the number square. Multiples of 9 are shaded.

1	2	3	4	5	6	7	8	9	10
11	12	13	14	15	16	17	18	19	20
21	22	23	24	25	26	27	28	29	30
31	32	33	34	35	36	37	38	39	40
41	42	43	44	45	46	47	48	49	50
51	52	53	54	55	56	57	58	59	60
61	62	63	64	65	66	67	68	69	70
71	72	73	74	75	76	77	78	79	80
81	82	83	84	85	86	87	88	89	90
91	92	93	94	95	96	97	98	99	100

Each snake has 9 sections. Add enough snakes to make 54 sections.

$6 \times 9 = 54$

Each tree has 9 big leaves. Add enough trees to make 27 leaves.

$3 \times 9 = 27$

Each lizard has 9 spikes. Add enough lizards to make 36 spikes.

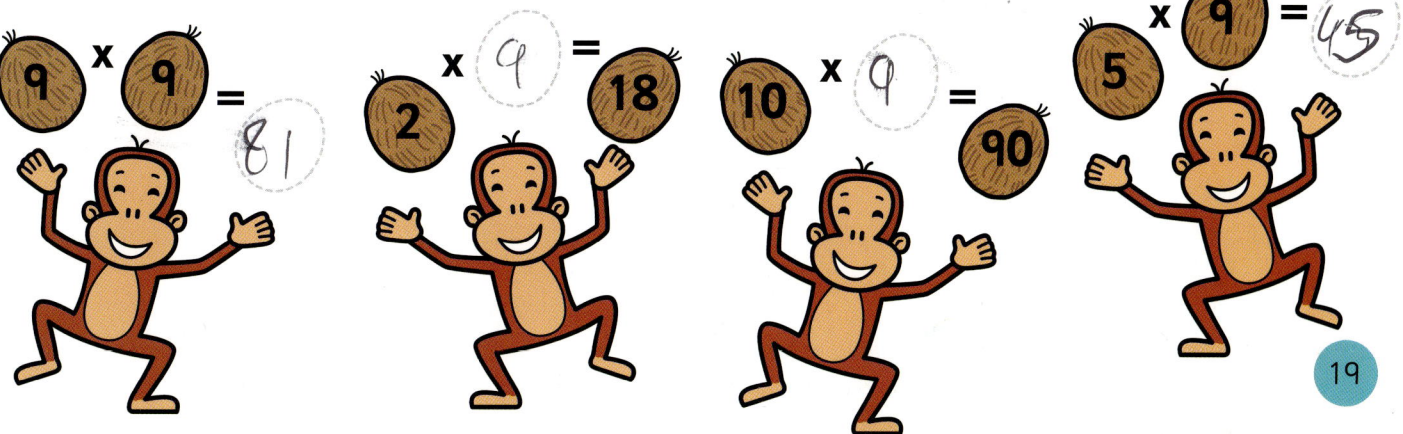

$4 \times 9 = 36$

Find the right sticker for each coconut.

$9 \times 9 = 81$

$2 \times 9 = 18$

$10 \times 9 = 90$

$5 \times 9 = 45$

10 times table

Write in the missing numbers.

0 x 10 = 0
1 x 10 = 10
2 x 10 = 20
3 x 10 = 30
4 x 10 = 40
5 x 10 = 50

6 x 10 = 60
7 x 10 = 70
8 x 10 = 80
9 x 10 = 90
10 x 10 = 100

Find the right stickers to finish the number square. Multiples of 10 are shaded.

1	2	3	4	5	6	7	8	9	10
11	12	13	14	15	16	17	18	19	20
21	22	23	24	25	26	27	28	29	30
31	32	33	34	35	36	37	38	39	40
41	42	43	44	45	46	47	48	49	50
51	52	53	54	55	56	57	58	59	60
61	62	63	64	65	66	67	68	69	70
71	72	73	74	75	76	77	78	79	80
81	82	83	84	85	86	87	88	89	90
91	92	93	94	95	96	97	98	99	100

Each ruler is 10cm long. Add enough rulers to make 60cm.

6 × 10 = 60

Each pyramid has 10 bricks. Add enough pyramids to make 50 bricks.

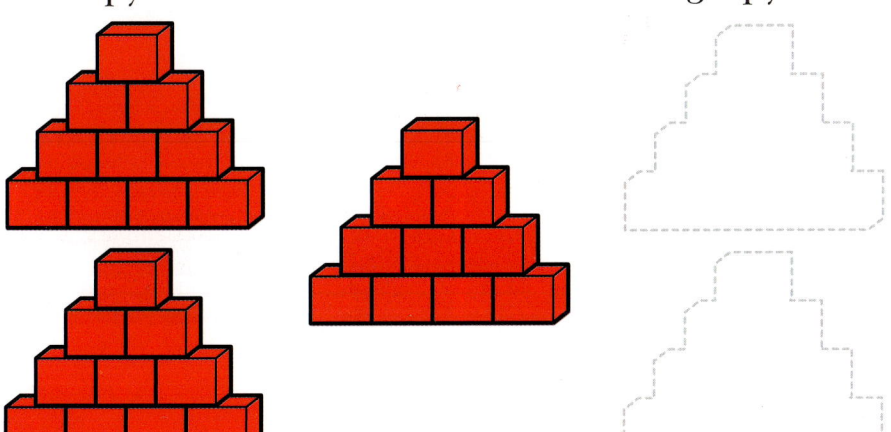

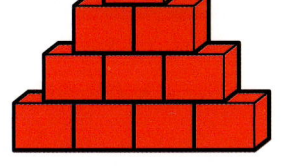

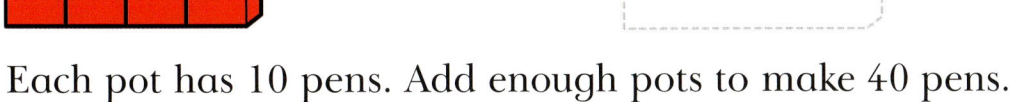

5 × 10 = 50

Each pot has 10 pens. Add enough pots to make 40 pens.

4 × 10 = 40

Find the correct sticker for each calculator.

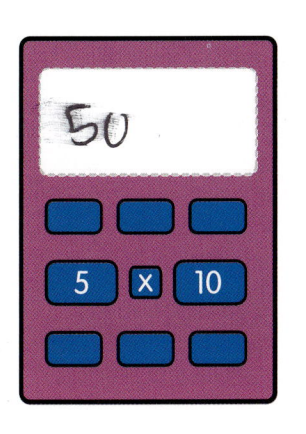

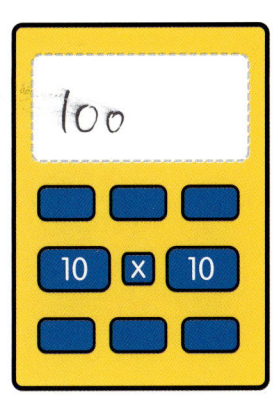

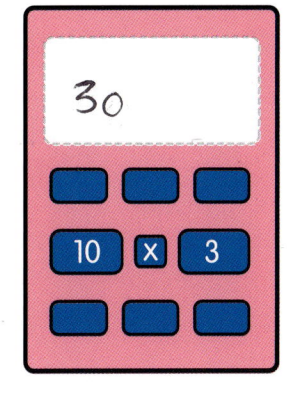

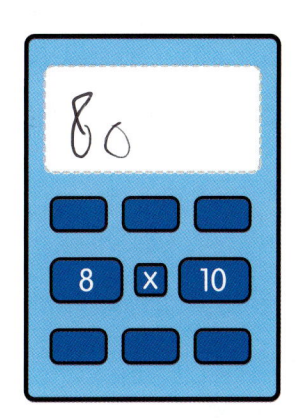

50	100	30	80
5 × 10	10 × 10	10 × 3	8 × 10

Tables fun

Can you find two planet stickers for each sun?

40   6   18

Find the correct stickers to finish the bubble number lines.

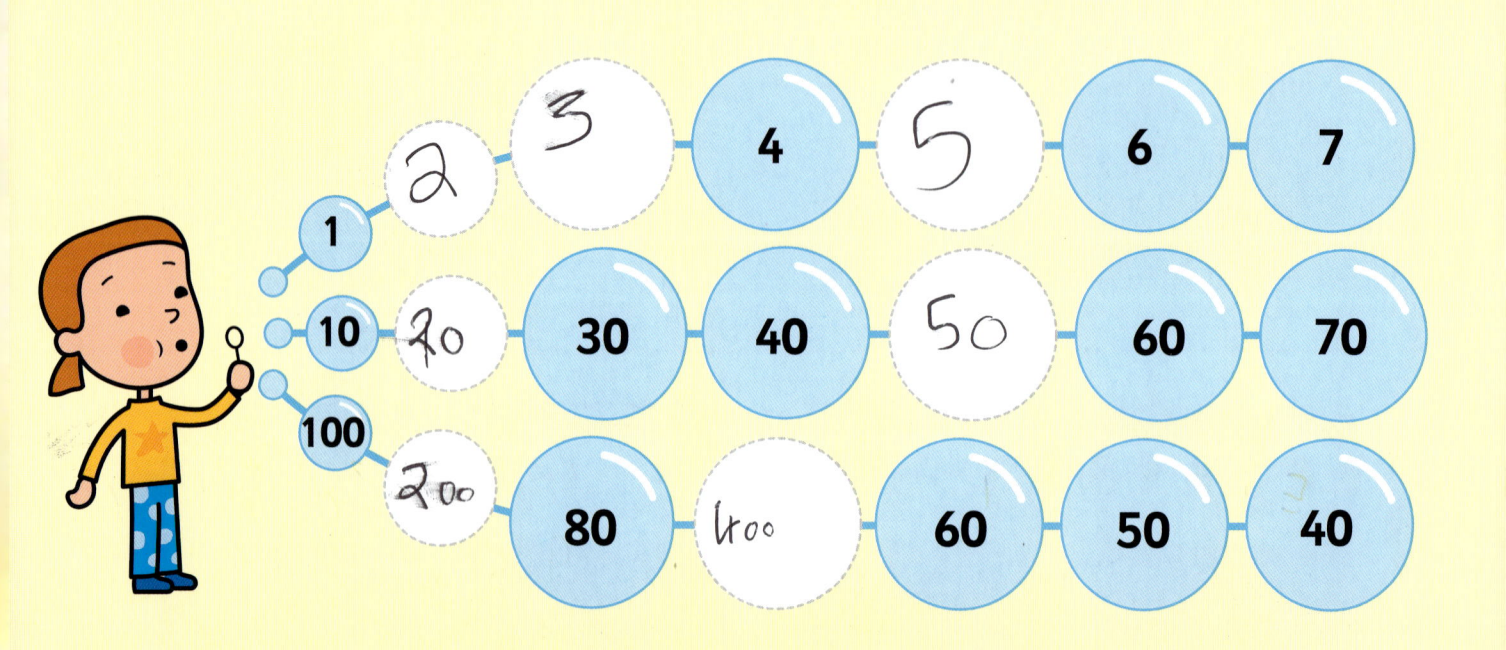

1 — 2 — 3 — 4 — 5 — 6 — 7

10 — 20 — 30 — 40 — 50 — 60 — 70

100 — 200 — 80 — 100 — 60 — 50 — 40

22

Finish the sums by writing the numbers.
8 biscuits shared by 2 people is 4 each.

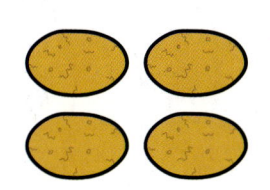

8 ÷ 2 = 4

12 cherries shared by 4 people is 3 each.

12 ÷ 4 = 3

9 carrots shared by 3 rabbits is 3 each.

9 ÷ 3 = 3

Write the correct number to answer these sums.

3 x 4 = 12   6 x 5 = 30   16 ÷ 4 = 4

Reward chart

This is your reward chart to keep a record of your progress. Each time you finish an activity, reward yourself with a star.

How many can you get?

★ 1 times table   ★ 2 times table

★ 3 times table   ★ 4 times table

★ 5 times table   ★ 6 times table

★ 7 times table   ★ 8 times table

★ 9 times table   ★ 10 times table

★ Number square stickers

★ Number lines   ★ Sharing out

★ Yes, I am really good at my times tables!